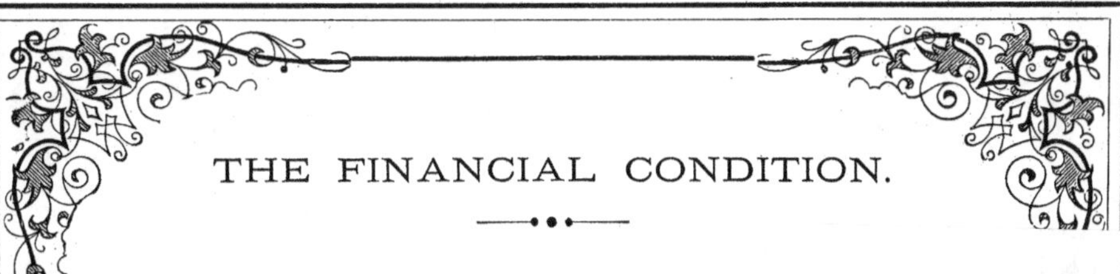

THE FINANCIAL CONDITION.

SPEECH

OF

WILLIAM SPRAGUE

IN THE

SENATE OF THE UNITED STATES,

MARCH 15, 1869.

NEW-YORK:
JOHN A. GRAY & GREEN, PRINTERS, 16 AND 18 JACOB STREET.
1869.

THE FINANCIAL CONDITION.

SPEECH

OF

WILLIAM SPRAGUE,

IN THE

SENATE OF THE UNITED STATES,

MARCH 15, 1869.

THE FINANCIAL CONDITION.

Mr. President: It is not my intention this morning to make a speech, or to enter into the discussion of this question by any show of statistics, or any details that will weary the Senate, or be tedious to my listeners. I have thought of this subject of finance with a great deal of anxiety. I have brought to bear upon its consideration the position in which the industries of the country are placed. I have compared those industries with the industries of other countries, and I have also compared the plan of finance which governs and controls our affairs with the plans of finance which govern and control the affairs of other countries. And, sir, I am weighed down with anxiety when I contemplate the ruin in store for us, unless we pause in the forced policy we have been pursuing since the close of the war.

When the Duke of Wellington conceived the idea that the English troops could fight in two ranks, and thereby, in his judgment, overcome the masses of French infantry, then domineering and triumphing over all Europe, he became tired and weary in the contemplation of that subject, and, obtaining leave of absence from the Indian government, reported himself at home and obtained employment. And with that simple idea in his head, he stationed himself in the Peninsula, and with the troops of whom he had charge, and the fortifications he found it necessary to build, he pursued his idea, and triumphed in his turn over Napoleon, who had subjugated Europe and triumphed over the best generals that the allies could bring to bear. I mention this to show that there are little things which govern the greatest of human affairs.

A few weeks since, in order to understand something of the condition of the South, I visited Georgia, and naturally was invited to inspect a cotton-mill. In the city of Augusta, Georgia, is a cotton-mill that to-day will surpass, and does surpass, in the success of its operations, the best one in New-England; and the secret of that success lies in the turn of one roll where the cotton is delivered on the spindle; it turning one hundred and fifteen turns to the minute, while others in New-England, and even by the side of it, turn ninety or one hundred.

Columbus, after he had discovered America, was asked at a festive board how, among all the people of his time, he should have discovered the New World. He asked them to stand an egg upon its end. They made every effort to accomplish the purpose, and, failing, looked to him. Cracking the egg on the end, it stood. It was sufficient; they understood him. Now, I send to the chair my proposition of finance, and ask that it be read. I do not offer it as an amendment, but simply as a paper on which, and on which alone, in my opinion, the financial problem can be solved.

The VICE-PRESIDENT. The Secretary will read the paper.

The Chief Clerk read as follows:

That the President nominate, and by and with the advice and consent of the Senate appoint, a commissioner, a deputy commissioner, and twenty-four judges of finance, to be selected from among men of wide experience and marked skill in business, exclusive of those engaged in banking, to examine into the English system of finance, touching the reception and disbursement of the national income, and to report at the next session of Congress a plan for the reception of the national revenues into the Treasury and the disbursement thereof, and to disconnect from the Treasury its jurisdiction over national banks. This power vested in said commissioners shall be so directed as to obviate the scarcity of money and high rates of interest, caused by the withdrawal of Treasury revenues from the market, by keeping daily in the market the same sum as is received into the Treasury, and to place the same on the market at such points as will check the increasing rates of interest, and increase capital while decreasing the cost thereof.

MR. SPRAGUE. It will be seen by that paper that my opinion is not favorable to an increased issue of legal tenders or of national bank currency. It will also be seen that I am not in favor of a repudiation of the national debt. But, sir, I do not sympathize with that class of men who are holding up to the gaze of the people of the United States the sacredness of that debt. I was opposed in your caucus, Mr. President, to an amendment of the Constitution giving undue protection to that debt, and I am also now opposed to any reiterated protection by the law contemplated by the bill before the Senate. I do not think that there is much sacredness in the issue of bonds for the Pacific Railroad, which has become a part of your national debt; and I see nothing sacred in the thousand and one unnecessary appropriations constantly made at each session of Congress.

The great bulk of the debt of the nation has been created in pursuance of a necessary and important object, that of maintaining the territorial integrity of the United States. In Great Britain to-day, the profits on almost any one of her great industries—her commerce, her manufactures of iron, or of coal, or of cotton, or of wool—are sufficient to pay the interest on her national debt. But is it the part of a people to drift into the condition of Mexican society, where the national debt is an oppressive burden to the community? If those whose business it is to make light the public burdens neglect, either from ignorance or from any other cause, to pursue a policy that will relieve instead of a policy that will destroy, if the people of this country are to-day, in consequence of the public debt bearing heavily upon them, drifting, as I verily believe, into the condition of Spanish and Mexican society, would any one demand that state of slavery rather than a cancelation of the debt?

Sir, you have provided for wholesale repudiation of private debts by your enactments at recent sessions of Congress. You can cancel debts between individuals, between the citizens of the country; but you look with holy horror upon a suggestion that if you pursue a policy of destruction this incubus will be sloughed off.

The Senate must know facts connected with the industries of this country. I told you, two years ago, that you had lost, or would lose if you were not exceedingly careful in reference to your future legislation, your monopoly of cotton, and nobody believed it; nobody will believe it now; but let me tell you that you have lost forever your sea-island cotton. Go to the South and make inquiries there. It is a thing that was, and the whole South is to-day trying to find a substitute in the rami or China grass, that will grow more prolifically, whereby they can replace that which has been lost. I tell you, sir, that in five years under the system of finance pursued by the projectors of this bill, that which of itself was a monopoly and has now ceased to be a monopoly, will cease to be a profitable business to those who are engaged in it. It may be that some of my friends from the South are watching the encroachments made upon that interest in Egypt, in India, and in Brazil.

The last statement from England of the receipts of that fibre shows a marvelous increase; one half of the cotton used by Great Britain is to-day received from Egypt, India, and Brazil; and the cotton produced by India, by Egypt, and by Brazil, is equal for all necessary purposes to that produced in this country.

But I have another point to urge upon the Western men of this Senate; it is that the boasted strength and prosperity of that section is but a shadow; and I point to the reports of the production of one article which is but a representative of all the others, wheat. It is the deliberate judgment of men who have statistics in their hands and are acquainted with this subject, that in the old States, on the old lands, exclusive of California, five bushels per acre is the amount of the crop on the average produced in the Western States, and that, including California and all the new lands that are taken up, eleven and a half bushels to the acre is the outside figure. What is the production of England, Ireland, and Scotland? Twenty-eight bushels per acre. Now, let me ask what prospect there is of the farming interest of this country competing in the markets of Europe? Sir, I do not care how large a product may be made by the American producer, if it costs him more than he gets for the article he produces, there is no wealth to him and no wealth to the nation.

It is within my own experience that the capital required to do the same business in this country beyond that required by the man doing a similar business in Great Britain, is more than three and a half times as much; and I illustrate it in this way: The English manufacturer plies his spindle at eighty cents, and does his business upon a capital to employ that spindle of eighty cents; the American manufacturer is compelled to employ a capital of $2.75 for a single spindle.

That is answer enough as to whether the volume of currency per head here, if equal to the volume of currency per head in Europe, is sufficient for this country. That is but one illustration; but it illustrates the whole business of the country, mechanical, farming, and manufacturing. It is a case in point and illustrates the whole. Every thing is in just that situation.

I will give you another instance to complete the picture. We make horse-shoes in this country, and it costs, without counting the capital invested, five cents per pound for each shoe. I can go to Canada and have them made for two cents per pound. The disparity is two cents there against five cents in this country. Is it known to the Senate, or to any body, that in every article that is produced in this country, whether it is an article of mechanics, manufactures, or agriculture, a very large element of the cost is the price paid for capital? Take, for instance, corn at fifty cents a bushel. Two thirds of that fifty cents is the cost of the capital employed in the production of that bushel of corn.

Every body in this country is willing to admit that we are wanting in capital, and that any measure which will tend to create capital in this country is that which is desirable beyond all other things. Now, I tell the Senate and I tell the people of this country, that the policy pursued from the beginning, of contraction and a constant indorsing of a public debt, has in effect driven capital from this country, made that which was scarce still scarcer, ruined your commerce, your manufacturing, and your farming, and even the bankers themselves, who are now constantly at your bar begging for some help—even they, eating their own words, admit that they are losing from day to day the business in which they were heretofore engaged, and they are giving it up by force to such interlopers as Fisk and Gould, and can not help themselves. They are tied hand and foot as surely and as certainly as they have tied this Senate and this country; for who ever heard of a policy that would drive a public debt or a private debt into the hands of the people of other countries? Why, sir, that absurd doctrine was given up two hundred and fifty years ago. In Elizabeth's time, the whole people of Great Britain were agreed that the public debt was a capital, and the interest from time to time paid on that debt should go to increase the capital within the territory of Great Britain, and by that increase her industries became more prosperous. But, sir, on the other hand, we have been trying to force beyond our borders the very thing on which and by which alone we are able to do our business. Bonds, currency, interest, are capital, and you can not separate one from the other.

But, sir, look and see what you have done with the banking capital of this country. It is an interesting subject to contemplate. There are $420,000,000 of national banking capital, and what have you done with it? I will show you. Three hundred and forty million dollars are locked up in your Treasury as security for circulation; $37,000,000 are locked up to secure deposits; there are $36,000,000 of bonds otherwise; there are $20,000,000 of other stocks and bonds. Then a large amount of the capital, in the shape of legal tenders, compound interest notes, and three per cent certificates, is compelled by law to be hoarded in the banks.

This whole capital, with from sixty to eighty millions besides, is forced into a dark corner. All there is now on which the industries of this people can be conducted is what little national bank currency there is afloat and the Government legal tenders, which by statute are constantly being reduced and hid away in the vaults of the banks. The interest that is paid by the borrower to-day is just double what it was at the close of the war.

I have said that the capital required by the farmer and the mechanic in this country, over that which is required in Great Britain, is three and a half times. Add to that the double rate of interest, and it is unnecessary that you shall pursue your inquiries one step further to understand exactly where the evil is in your financial management. It is just there and nowhere else. Great Britain's system of railroads, based upon her low interest and abundant capital, will carry a ton of coal one hundred miles for what it costs me in this country to carry a ton of coal three miles. I pay for carrying a ton three miles as much as the manufacturer in Great Britain pays for transporting it one hundred miles.

All these things are true; there is no mistake in one of them; and there is no necessity whatever to surmise or to speculate as to what is the cause of the present disturbance in business. Go ask any distributor of goods in New-York or Boston what is the condition of their accounts for the past three years touching the payments of the debts made by the West, and there is not one of them who can show that he could pay his interest and his rents. There is not one of them who, if he tells you the truth, will not say that he is in debt; the poor debts that have been made, the failures that have occurred, have been greater than all the profits made from business; and they will tell you again, that the securities otherwise in their possession are weakened twenty per cent.

How long, I ask, can a country pursue that sort of business and be assured at all that it can maintain any value for its public debt? Some people — and there are such here in the Senate, perhaps—will say that the recent advance of your bonds in Europe was caused by the proposition now before the body. There are some people who will believe even that that is the fact. Well, sir, if it is any satisfaction for them to know it, I can state that at the same time, and from the same cause, the Government bonds of Turkey assumed a similar relation as to price; they advanced about six or seven per cent. The cause of it was simply that the English capitalists had taken two or three per cent long enough, and they were willing to take greater risks and obtain securities that would pay a higher rate of interest.

Some people, too, will say that the rise in the value of your currency was occasioned by some remark that has been made by somebody, or some resolution before the bar of this Senate, or otherwise; that that was the cause of an increased value to your paper. What was the cause? This rise in the value of your securities drove them to Europe, and drove to Europe the capital on which your business was done, and exchange has been drawn against them, coming in competition with gold, and the result was inevitable. Sir, that was the cause, and no other. The idea of resolutions like this before the Senate or anywhere else, or articles in newspapers, or speeches made by any body, having an effect upon the price of gold or the value of your bonds, is the most complete absurdity that ever afflicted the brains of sensible men.

Congress and the Supreme Court seem to be acting in accord on this subject. My friend from Indiana [MR. MORTON] in his remarks the other day, told the Senate that the second section of the bill was in qualification of the dangerous influences connected with the recent decision of the Supreme Court. As my mind is not taken up with any of the ameliorating projects, or any of the medicines that are used to cure this disease, I had not paid any attention whatever to the merits of that section in detail; but it was the business of somebody to take some notice of it, and my friend from Indiana was correct in the judgment he gave, and the Senate, led by outside influences, by men who have given this question no study whatever, were wrong, and I will show you how. I read from the *Bankers' Gazette* of Friday, March 5th, 1869; bankers tell the truth sometimes:

> "Since the late legal tender decision of the Supreme Court authorizing contracts to pay coin, lenders feel more at liberty to demand coin interest, and the banks and conservative private bankers who heretofore have declined to accept more than seven per cent in currency, now feel less hesitation about asking gold rates when the condition of the market enables them to do so."

In the interest of high cost of interest, in the interest of protection to capital, the capital now absorbing all the best interests of this country, to destroy them. If I should say to any body that it is my deliberate judgment that this Government has failed in the object that it was intended by its projectors to secure, I suppose I should be scouted at. But, sir, when I compare the situation of this country to-day with the situation of that country from whence we sprung, I find that not only in capital, but in general intelligence, in education, in liberty among the people, they far exceed the privileges and the power of the people of this country. They are increasing in a ratio most astounding in education and in the refinements of life, as the statistics show. After the convulsions which racked this continent, and considering the intimate relations that subsist between this country and Great Britain, what was the effect of our war upon that nation? A simple Fenian commotion; and that was all. Look at her commanding one fifth of the territory and one fourth of the population of the globe; her commerce occupying prosperously and profitably every sea; her industry permeating and being introduced into every market in the world, standing strong, able, and powerful everywhere. And where are we? All we have to help ourselves in the world is our cotton, which we are about to lose, and our tobacco, which we shall lose.

My friend from California (Mr. Cole) will say that we have the production of gold. Sir, that bears the fortune of cotton, and wheat, and every thing else. You find in the gentleman's own State that the high price of capital and its scarcity, made so by your acts, have driven men from the production of gold into farming and wool raising. The paper I have before me shows and criticises the immense falling off in that production.

What, I ask, are you to rely upon to sustain the price of your public debt, when there is no profitable occupation for your people? Will this bulling operation that you have tried for the past three years have any effect? What will this proposition of curtailing the currency, in order to increase its value, effect? Nothing but the same old story: want of prosperity, want of employment, and a condition of national indebtedness like that of Mexico. Why not have made an effort to restore prosperity to all the branches of your industry on which to have floated your debt and maintained its price, rather than, by constitutional amendments and by statute law, be constantly making an effort to bull up the price of your national securities, driving what little capital there was left into their investment, and depriving every industry of the necessary means to carry it on?

I do not sympathize at all with any of these projects for paying the five-twenties in greenbacks or legal tenders, because that will be depriving the Government of full value for what they gave, and it will be robbing the people; for the introduction of an additional amount of currency, not heretofore well settled, not heretofore permeating through all the avenues of business and trade, will, for the time being, depreciate the value of all, and that capital being the only capital that the people hold, they would be robbed by any such increase of issue. If those whose business it is to look well into this question, will examine the policy pursued by Morris when closing up the business of the Confederation after the Revolution, or by Hamilton in reconstructing the finances on the formation of the Constitution, or by Dallas when correcting the evils growing out of the war of 1814, and will embody upon our system the theory and practice established by those men, the country will ask for nothing better.

The country and its business interests were prostrated to the very dust three months ago by the retirement of $6,000,000 of currency by speculators in New-York through Fisk and others; and yet last month there was drawn into the Treasury $13,000,000 more than was distributed to the country—enough to stagger even the strength and stability of Britain's finances. No nation under heaven can stand that draught upon it, can stand the scarcity produced by that result. And yet people wonder why we are so affected by the rise and fall of gold; and we say it is owing to the fact that we are not paying specie. Sir, if you forced yourself into a condition of the payment of specie to-morrow, you would not have benefited your position one iota. The same scarcity of capital, the same high rates of interest, would exist then as exist now; and that condition of things being so, you could not raise wheat in the West, we could not manufacture in the East, and we should have nothing to do to employ our commerce, nothing whatever to give to our flag on the sea.

It is said that the tariff is the cause of these high prices. I deny it. If you will give to me a system in your Treasury that will let the money out of it at a given rate as fast as it is received, I, for one, will pledge myself to advocate the repeal of all your tariff laws in five years. We ask for nothing in this country, in my judgment, but the reception of the revenues upon the market to control capital in the interest of abundance and a lower rate of interest. Give me that, and I will be your strongest advocate for a repeal of all your tariff acts.

We condemn speculators, and gold gamblers, and stock-jobbers. I have been led into that error myself. But, sir, those gentlemen but occupy the position that they have been taught to occupy, and they avail themselves of a perfectly legitimate trade and business. The fault is, that the Congress of the United States, under bad advisers, leave open the opportunities for money-making in that department, inducing the people of the whole country who have capital to employ their means in those operations, withdrawing them from the business interes s ofthe country. Sir, you set the example of speculation when you, in order to create a better value for your legal tenders, make them scarce. What more have Drew, and Fisk, and Gould done?—and yet you condemn them. What more did Vanderbilt do, when he convulsed the market in his efforts to place Harlem where he did? You do the same thing exactly, under the sacred sanction of law and in behalf of a great people. You are a stock-jobber and a gold gambler, as much as any one of them.

If the country is prosperous, why is it that you are convulsed with failures and bankruptcies? Why are your newspapers and your courts filled day by day in every village, in every town, and in every city of this country with accounts of bankruptcies? There were twenty-six hundred failures in 1867, twenty-six hundred failures in 1868, and God only knows what will be the extent of them for 1869.

It is said that the Parliament of Charles II. was more successful than any of its predecessors. It was in consequence of its repealing most of the laws that had been enacted centuries before. This Congress may with profit follow its example. They will do well to look back, and take back the acts which have tied up the capital of the country, or forced it beyond the uses of its people.

I did not intend, Mr. President, when I rose to my feet this morning, to occupy the time of the Senate so long; and I beg pardon for having done so; but the subject has worn upon me, and the thought of the condition to which this country is certainly drifting, and the fact that those around me would not listen, nor will they believe what is the true condition of the country at the present time, the fact that no impression can be made upon any body about me, makes me sick at heart and almost unable to move. I would not have occupied the attention of the Senate for a moment, if that condition of things did not exist. Sir, if there was any credit, or if there was any advantage to the country in the position taken by me in the beginning of this war, if the force of that example amounted to any thing, or if I have ever done any thing in the course of my life of advantage to the country, this of giving the exact condition in which the country is placed, transcends them all.

The Dutch said to the English somewhere about the middle of the sixteenth century, "So long as you are jealous of our financial policy, we shall continue to be mistress of the seas; we shall continue to do the manufacturing and the weaving for the continent and for the world." When the Dutchman succeeded to the throne of James, after the revolution of 1688, England obtained the Dutch system, and from a power less than Holland at that time, with an income not as great as that of Holland, and not one fourth that of France, in thirty years she triumphed over them all. Preëminent stand William of Orange and William of Nassau—one giving liberty to his country in his contest with Charles V.; the other giving liberty, civilization, power, to the English nation superior to that of any nation, ancient or modern.

I have illustrated in two or three little things to show that it was the most trifling appendage almost to your Treasury that had determined all these things; and if I can call the attention of Senators to that one point, and if they will look at it as they look at any other subject which occupies their minds, they will give to their country a position equal to that now held by England with every other advantage beyond that of any people in the world. With this financial system fully established, the career of this people in development in every direction will be the wonder of this age and of this period.

Sir, I do not expect to influence the passage of this measure. I tell the Senate that every word that I have said as to either what is or what it is to be, may be relied upon. There can be no mistake in the things that I have given, because they have been found established on facts, upon the exact situation in which things are. I could give the record for them all, but I forbear; I know they will not be read. If, therefore, I have drawn attention in a different direction from what has been heretofore given to the Senate, it is because I have studied this subject in the direction through which Great Britain has obtained her successes, and by which we can obtain similar successes. I know of no other way to understand a question, than to compare the condition of things in a country embarrassed, with the condition of things in a country that is prosperous. I ask attentive consideration of the suggestions I have made, not expecting to embarrass particularly the passage of this measure, but still being opposed to it as being similar in its character and tendencies to the whole financial system which has embarrassed the country for the past three years.

www.ingramcontent.com/pod-product-compliance
Lightning Source LLC
LaVergne TN
LVHW010833120826
845149LV00016B/1362
* 9 7 8 1 4 1 8 1 9 0 7 7 4 *